A

AF538492

New

To Bob and Jack —
All my love
and best wishes
to you!
Carolyne
12/30/99

Resonance

A New Resonance

Emerging Voices in English-Language Haiku

Bachini • Chang • Connor • Elliott
Giesecke • Gilliland • gordon • Howard
Jensen • Kaur • Ketchek • Lippy
Missias • Ogoshi • Partridge • Patrick
Rohrig • Stefanac • Watsky • Young

Edited by

Jim Kacian & Dee Evetts

Red Moon Press

A New Resonance:

Emerging Voices in English-Language Haiku

Copyright©1999
ISBN 1-893959-03-1

Red Moon Press
P.O. Box 2461
Winchester VA
22504-1661 USA
redmoon@shentel.net

Special thanks to
Maureen Gorman
for her help
in the preparation
of this volume.

Cover Painting:
Stepping Out by Gail Foster
66" x 50", Oil & Beeswax on Canvas
Used by Permission.

Foreword

A poem reveals: a poet is revealed. Information accumulates, parameters become apparent. We grow to know the situations and circumstances which the poems describe. But through the voice of the poet, we come to know more than facts: we come to know the human element of these facts, how the poet figures into the situation, how he feels about being there, how she acts in accordance. The poems are a way into the situation. The voice is the guide to how the poet sees and deals with it.

Assembled here is a substantial body of work by twenty different poets. Most of the circumstances of their lives distinguish them from one another: they come from three different continents, and from far across the wide expanse of this country; they are professionals and day laborers, educators, mystics. They are single and married, male and female, formal and informal. But they hold in common some things which recommend them to us: a clear eye; an ability to capture what they see accurately and with verve; a fondness for a brief form of poetry which they have found to be expressive and revelatory.

Our regard for these poets has risen through this deeper contact with them and their work. We think, as you come to know them better, you will be as pleased to know them as we are.

Jim Kacian & Dee Evetts, Editors

A New Resonance

Emerging Voices in English-Language Haiku

Bachini

Chang
Connor
Elliott
Giesecke
Gilliland
gordon
Howard
Jensen
Kaur
Ketchek
Lippy
Missias
Ogoshi
Partridge
Patrick
Rohrig
Stefanac
Watsky
Young

Annie Bachini
ESL Teacher

Born 23 July 1950
London, England
Currently resides
London, England

We know at once Bachini is British, and we quickly come to recognize her roots in the inner city—the sights, the sounds, the circumstances which present themselves to her on a daily basis. And we discover her responses to this demanding, occasionally hostile environment: a certain nostalgia, a kind of bravery to see things through, and a willingness to adapt and allow it to extend her tastes and horizons.

Credits

after the spring clean: *Blithe Spirit 7:4*
day after day: *Presence 9*
sale: *Presence 7*
vibrating: *unpublished*
bits of poster: *Frogpond XXI:3*
only the cacti remain: *Frogpond XXI:3*
in the formal garden: *Presence 3*
after dad: *Presence 4*
interview: *unpublished*
background jazz: *poetry postcard quarterly*
a smiling soldier: *Blithe Spirit 5:1*
a strand of hair: *Haïku sans frontières*
breadcrumbs: *Haïku sans frontières*
sweeping the garden: *Blithe Spirit 7:4*
sound of laughter: *Mainichi Daily News*

after dad appeared in *The Iron Book of British Haiku*
a smiling soldier appeared as an example
in "The Conscious Eye" in *Frogpond XXI:1*

after the spring clean
wishing I'd played the music box
one last time

day after day
bits of the chained bicycle
disappear

sale:
'fill a bag for £1'
suddenly my taste broadens

vibrating
with the pneumatic drill
arm tattoo

bits of poster
and station mould
map out unknown regions

only the cacti remain:
the café changed
to a hi-fi shop

in the formal garden
children play
hide-and-seek

after dad
tidies her scarf
the toddler fixes it herself

interview—
the space between me
and the panel

background jazz—
on his mobile phone
a man walks to and fro

a smiling soldier
caught at war—flashes his knife
for the camera

a strand of hair
unfolds
with the letter

breadcrumbs cupped in my hand—
the last notes of an opera

sweeping the garden
I forget about my landlord's
latest threats

sound of laughter
from behind the wall—
the geraniums in bloom

Bachini

Chang

Connor

Elliott

Giesecke

Gilliland

gordon

Howard

Jensen

Kaur

Ketchek

Lippy

Missias

Ogoshi

Partridge

Patrick

Rohrig

Stefanac

Watsky

Young

Yu Chang
College Professor

Born 30 August 1938
Ichang, Hupei, China
Currently resides
Schenectady, New York

It is not Chang's interest in nature, but rather his interaction with it, that is most evident from his work. He has a keen sense of the interface between human habitation and the natural world/environment, and some of his most delightful moments derive from a sense of being part of the picture. He is also a painter with words, and the sensuality of his writing is evident in many of these poems.

Credits

warm rain: *Frogpond XXI:1*
rest stop: *Frogpond XXI:2*
faint stars: *Modern Haiku XXIX:3*
parting her pink robe: *unpublished*
bumble bee: *Acorn 1*
still thinking of her: *Modern Haiku XXVIII:1*
summer twilight: *Modern Haiku XXVII:3*
stepping out: *unpublished*
almost dusk: *Modern Haiku XXX:2*
a scorpion emerges: *Modern Haiku XXIX:1*
starry night: *Frogpond XXI:1*
the sharpness: *Frogpond XXI:3*
pebbled beach: *Acorn 2*
sheets: *South by Southeast 3:4*
first frost: *unpublished*

faint stars won the 3rd Shiki Internet Kukai 1997
summer twilight appeared in *The Red Moon Anthology 1996*
starry night won a Museum of Haiku Literature Award 1998

warm rain
the spring moon returns
to the rusty can

rest stop—
a walkman atop
the milestone marker

faint stars—
the flapping of canvas
on the grape truck

parting her pink robe
—daybreak

bumblebee
deeper in the petunia
summer heat

still thinking of her
the sticky threads
of the severed lotus root

summer twilight
the red barn's roof line
sags with age

stepping out
with my holey socks
summer stars

almost dusk—
the raspberry stalk bends
with a purple finch

a scorpion emerges
from a pile of chilies
—desert sunset

starry night—
biting into a melon
full of seeds

the sharpness
of the white picket fence
—gray morning

pebbled beach—
how carefully she chooses
her words

sheets
on the clothesline
the wind curves

first frost
a homeless man appears
in the new development

Bachini
Chang

Connor

Elliott
Giesecke
Gilliland
gordon
Howard
Jensen
Kaur
Ketchek
Lippy
Missias
Ogoshi
Partridge
Patrick
Rohrig
Stefanac
Watsky
Young

Pamela Connor
Gallery Owner

Born 23 November 1944
Rockville Centre, New York
Currently resides
Luzerne, Pennsylvania

There are two key elements pervading much of Connor's work: a constant awareness of mortality as part of the human condition, and an overriding compassion for the living which arises from this awareness. She takes particular delight in the actions of children, with an intense yet objective eye that informs her poems with a vitality and appreciation.

Credits

heat wave: *unpublished*
twisted: *South by Southeast 5:3*
planting them: *unpublished*
spring cleaning: *unpublished*
morning sunshine: *unpublished*
convent cemetery: *Brussels Sprout XII:1*
splashes of it: *Climbing the Flame Tree*
heat wave: *Frogpond XXI:3*
turning the double play: *Frogpond XXI:2*
the heat: *Climbing the Flame Tree*
my simple uncle: *Modern Haiku XXVI:1*
Hallowe'en: *Modern Haiku XXX:1*
in sin: *Frogpond XVII:4*
snow angels: *unpublished*
wrapping myself: *unpublished*

planting them and *in sin* received Citations
in the Jessee Poetry Contest 1998
splashes of it was Highly Commended
and *the heat* Commended in the New Zealand
1998 International Poetry Competition

heat wave . . .
the gravedigger lays his lunch
on white marble

twisted
into the sheets
March wind

planting them
on her death anniversary
early potatoes

spring cleaning
an unmarked box
filled with mother's smell

morning sunshine . . .
the jingle of coins
in my pocket

convent cemetery
small slate headstones
row after row

splashes of it
on the summer breeze—
children's voices

heat wave:
gift from a playmate
her lopsided haircut

turning the double play—
her perfect pirouette
around second base

the heat—
slipping inside the cool
of the old church

my simple uncle
no wisdom lines
on his aged face

Hallowe'en . . .
hanging plastic spiders
in real webs

in sin—
Amish child makes a face
on her doll

snow angels
almost invisible
under new snow

wrapping myself
into my dead father's shirt—
favorite shade of blue

Bachini
Chang
Connor

Elliott

Giesecke
Gilliland
gordon
Howard
Jensen
Kaur
Ketchek
Lippy
Missias
Ogoshi
Partridge
Patrick
Rohrig
Stefanac
Watsky
Young

David Elliott
College Professor

Born 26 December 1944
Minneapolis, Minnesota
Currently resides
Factoryville, Pennsylvania

Elliott's poems show him to be a hiker, gardener, outdoorsman; equally, they show him to be a practiced hand at haiku. There is an assurance and a range which mark his familiarity with the form. But he remains attentive to the journey: there is also awareness of life's precariousness, as well as tenacity in meeting and dealing with it. His work shows a sensitivity to being near the edge always, but never without a sense of resource.

Credits

Light rain: *Modern Haiku*
All these weeks: *Brussels Sprout*
The roto-tiller: *Haiku Canada Newsletter*
Even over here: *Frogpond*
Board meeting: *Frogpond*
No one answers: *Modern Haiku*
My son's x-ray: *Brussels Sprout*
Nurses' Station: *Frogpond*
Trying to follow: *Modern Haiku*
The hike slows: *Point Judith Light*
Breaking camp: *Modern Haiku*
September twilight: *Ko*
Not expecting: *Heiwa: Peace Poetry in English and Japanese*
My head on her breast: *Brussels Sprout*
Shielding his eyes: *Modern Haiku*

Shielding his eyes appeared in *The Haiku Anthology*

Light rain
a woman reading braille
on the porch

All these weeks
my bootprints
frozen in the mud

The roto-tiller
stalls
tree frogs in the distance

Even over here
under the broccoli
a squash runner

Board meeting
wasps caught
between the windows

No one answers . . .
between the rings
faint laughter

My son's x-ray
clamped to the light
cowlick faintly visible

Nurses' Station—
above the heart monitors
a soap opera

Trying to follow
a kite string down
to the right kid

the hike slows
to a halt—
wild raspberries

Breaking camp . . .
beside the fireplace a mushroom
just poking through

September twilight
a spider crosses the pile
of newly dug potatoes

Not expecting
such a moon
over my crabby neighbor's roof

My head on her breast
hearing her heart skip
the furnace kicks in

Shielding his eyes
with his baseball glove
    first geese

Bachini
Chang
Connor
Elliott

Giesecke

Gilliland
gordon
Howard
Jensen
Kaur
Ketchek
Lippy
Missias
Ogoshi
Partridge
Patrick
Rohrig
Stefanac
Watsky
Young

Lee Giesecke

Actuary

Born 12 November 1938
Kansas City, Missouri
Currently resides
Annandale, Virginia

Humor, usually self-deprecating, is the first and most obvious endearment of Giesecke's work. This can make it easy to miss some of his other qualities. A deeply-felt empathy, and joy in human interchange, underpin that humor and provide the substance of his best poems. Not exclusively an observer of human foibles, he shows a strong attraction to nature, with a special fondness for the unusual or exotic moment of beauty.

Credits

New Year's Day: *Modern Haiku XXIX:1*
luminescent bay: *unpublished*
from my sparkler: *Modern Haiku XXIX:2*
wife asleep: *unpublished*
wistfully she touches: *Modern Haiku XVI:1*
dry well: *Acorn 1*
swift: *unpublished*
fast: *Modern Haiku XVII:1*
reading Jane Austin: *unpublished*
after joining: *unpublished*
zoo escape: *unpublished*
searching the field book: *unpublished*
somehow the horse: *unpublished*
ice film on the stream: *unpublished*
intensive care: *Frogpond XIX:3*

intensive care appeared in *The Red Moon Anthology 1997*

New Year's Day—
a man with a weight set
staggers to his car

luminescent bay
the trace from the stone
I throw in

from my sparkler
yours lit
on your face the glow

wife asleep—
in the darkened mirror
my sweater sparks

wistfully she touches
her lover's
vasectomy

dry well
the dropped stone's

thud

swift—
the flipped-wing scull
of his turn

fast
wasn't it
she complained

reading Jane Austin
finding myself
unduly civil

after joining
our Malamutes' howls
all of us feeling fresh

zoo escape—
below the autumn sky
a lone green balloon

searching the field book—
it seems I'm holding
poison sumac

somehow the horse
leaves in my hand
this little 'Gala' sticker

ice film on the stream—
over the leaf dam
a trickle of sound

intensive care—
from the new patient
a whispered *damn*

Bachini
Chang
Connor
Elliott
Giesecke

Gilliland

gordon
Howard
Jensen
Kaur
Ketchek
Lippy
Missias
Ogoshi
Partridge
Patrick
Rohrig
Stefanac
Watsky
Young

Robert Gilliland
Psychiatrist

Born 14 December 1946
Galveston, Texas
Currently resides
Austin, Texas

There is an unmistakeable vitality to these poems, a vegetative creeping quality. They are composed of things which grow and fill and decay, which shift constantly, if almost imperceptibly, and by so doing mark the boundaries of the space they inhabit: cows fill a shadow, vines a work area. This luxuriating in the natural cycle refreshes us, while at the same time models our own rise and decline. It holds the moment of stasis—so often caught here—as one of elegant yet transitory poise.

Credits

sudden shower: *unpublished*
in the compost pile: *Frogpond XIX:2*
old boundary fence: *unpublished*
roadside stand: *Modern Haiku XXIX:3*
pale summer sky: *Frogpond XX:2*
dusk: *Frogpond XXI:2*
midsummer heat: *Tundra 1*
a tree long dead: *Modern Haiku XXVIII:1*
late afternoon light: *A Solitary Leaf*
morning glory: *unpublished*
midsummer heat: *Frogpond XX:2*
autumn wind: *Modern Haiku XXVIII:3*
Indian Summer: *Modern Haiku XXX:2*
sound of the scissors: *Modern Haiku XXIX:2*
slow shower of leaves: *unpublished*

old boundary fence received Honorable Mention
in the Kiyoshi Tokutomi Memorial Haiku Contest 1998
autumn wind appeared in *The Red Moon Anthology 1997*
old boundary fence, roadside shade, midsummer heat, a tree long dead, pale summer sky, autumn wind, & sound of the scissors
appeared in *mosquitoes and moonlight*

sudden shower—
a tin roof steams
into the summer sky

in the compost pile
an onion
coming back to life

old boundary fence
  wound with morning glory
    past the county line

roadside stand . . .
between melon thumps the click
of farmers' dominos

pale summer sky—
an oak tree's shadow
fills with cows

dusk
the green vine's tendrils
round a fallen tree

midsummer heat—
trickle of the sewer pipe
feeding the creek

a tree long dead—
every branch abloom
with trumpet vine

late afternoon light—
in the clover two bees
trade places

morning glory—
winding up the handle of
a rusty mower

midsummer heat . . .
on the whitewashed fence
the white nail's shadow

autumn wind—
a brown bag still holding
the bottle's shape

Indian Summer
a co-worker's ivy
invades my cubicle

sound of the scissors
closing on a rose's stem—
autumn afternoon

slow shower of leaves . . .
black cat curled up
on the neighbor's shed

Bachini
Chang
Connor
Elliott
Giesecke
Gilliland

gordon

Howard
Jensen
Kaur
Ketchek
Lippy
Missias
Ogoshi
Partridge
Patrick
Rohrig
Stefanac
Watsky
Young

chris gordon

Graduate Student

Born 13 May 1966
Toronto, Canada
Currently resides
Oakland, California

A number of adjectives suggest themselves when we encounter this poet's work—edgy, sensual, even at times surreal. At his best, gordon gives us precise feelings and an uneasy feeling of slippage, not allowing us facile responses as he moves between one clearly defined state and another. This results in a feeling of intimacy—not as in the remove of autobiography, but rather in the way we come to know an author in the best of journal writing.

Credits

a purple evening: *Raw NervZ Haiku IV:1*
one sock still on: *Raw NervZ Haiku III:2*
balled up: *Lost and Found Times 41*
the drip: *Raw NervZ III:2*
dressing afterwards: *Raw NervZ II:2*
the hot asphalt roof: *Modern Haiku XXVI:2*
a hurried goodbye: *Caffeine 14*
the hot bus: *unpublished*
"bagpipes?": *unpublished*
my cold foot: *Modern Haiku XXV:2*
her hand covers: *Modern Haiku XXVI:2*
on the edge: *A Guide to Haiku for the 21st Century*
i buy another book: *Modern Haiku XXV:2*
a new moon: *Pagan Situation*
"will this be one . . .?": *Raw NervZ III:1*

a purple evening, the drip & my cold foot
appeared in *A Guide to Haiku for the 21st Century*
i buy another book appeared in *Haiku World*

a purple evening   in the window she folds her underwear

one sock still on   she's darker than i thought

balled up in the shower her wet dress   the soughing darkness the drip down the back of her thigh   a mourning dove calls

dressing afterwards   her voice hardens

the hot asphalt roof   small white petals blow in circles

a hurried goodbye   the chain link fence in both our mouths

the hot bus   a single hair grazes my ankle

"bagpipes?"   cutting roots into slices this first day of fall

my cold foot steps on her bra still warm

her hand covers my ear   the sound blood makes

on the edge of the paper an ant   the smell of rain without the rain

i buy another book about non-attachment

a new moon   the radio, barely audible, late at night

"will this be one of the days i remember?" and grass

Bachini
Chang
Connor
Elliott
Giesecke
Gilliland
gordon

Howard

Jensen
Kaur
Ketchek
Lippy
Missias
Ogoshi
Partridge
Patrick
Rohrig
Stefanac
Watsky
Young

Elizabeth Howard
English Teacher

Born 26 October 1933
Lebanon, Tennessee
Currently resides
Crossville, Tennessee

That Howard is a nature poet is abundantly clear. Her command of language often permits her to capture the importance of what otherwise might seem, without this exactitude, elusive or slight. This precision also permits her to enter her poems, unobtrusively but surely, often revealing a subtlety and humor that disguises her participation in, and not mere observation of, the destiny of the natural world.

Credits

snowy pasture: *Modern Haiku XXIX:2*
winter sunrise: *South by Southeast 4:2*
ancient rock wall: *Frogpond XX:3*
wind shrieking: *Northwest Literary Forum 24*
mountain evening: *Modern Haiku XXVI:3*
creek willows: *Frogpond XIX:2*
heat index rising: *Modern Haiku XXVII:1*
Indian mounds: *Modern Haiku XXIV:3*
the old truck's windshield: *Frogpond XXI:1*
meadowlarks circle: *South by Southeast 3:2*
evening shadows: *Modern Haiku XXIII:2*
deer tracks: *Modern Haiku XXIX:1*
the creek rising: *Modern Haiku XXVIII:3*
a wrinkled web: *Modern Haiku XXVIII:1*
the cellar door opened: *Modern Haiku XXVIII:3*

meadowlarks circle appeared in *The Red Moon Anthology 1996*
the creek rising appeared in *The Red Moon Anthology 1997*

snowy pasture—
a newborn calf's
erratic tracks

winter sunrise—
other suns in windows
across the hollow

ancient rock wall
under the layer of ice
the snail's summer trace

wind shrieking
the row of icicles
curves leeward

mountain evening
  a raven sweeps down the spill
  of daylilies

creek willows
  a yellow fishing fly
  in the spider's web

heat index rising
the scream of a red-tailed hawk
in the morning fog

Indian mounds—
a tribe of old men
launching model planes

the old truck's windshield—
multiple rainbows
in the spiderwebs

meadowlarks circle
the summer hayfield—
song ebbing and flowing

evening shadows—
nuclear and grain silos
become one

deer tracks
circle the drying pond—
heat lightning

the creek rising
a snake skin surges
in the rock's wash hole

a wrinkled web
shrouds the child's baseball—
the spider's eggs

the cellar door opened—
orange salamanders
flee the lantern

Bachini
Chang
Connor
Elliott
Giesecke
Gilliland
gordon
Howard

Jensen

Kaur
Ketchek
Lippy
Missias
Ogoshi
Partridge
Patrick
Rohrig
Stefanac
Watsky
Young

Jennifer Jensen

Technical Writer

Born 25 April 1964
Victoria, British Columbia
Currently resides
Fair Oaks, California

Jensen is new in the very best way—exploring the world with unsullied eyes. At the same time she is exploring the haiku form, which demands of her a heightened attention. We see her drawn particularly to moments of human interest, which are often expressed indirectly. There is also a sensitivity to fluctuations in the quality and flow of light, attributable perhaps to her Canadian origins.

Credits

spring rain: *evening thunder*
low tide: *unpublished*
Monday morning: *Frogpond XXI:2*
bowing low: *unpublished*
the sun's warmth: *unpublished*
summer storm: *unpublished*
washing up: *unpublished*
summer's end: *unpublished*
moon viewing party: *unpublished*
after the ambulance: *unpublished*
resting her head: *unpublished*
autumn rain: *unpublished*
approaching winter: *unpublished*
early darkness: *unpublished*
cluster of berries: *unpublished*

spring rain
above the dam
almost silence

low tide
among fishing herons
a child wades

Monday morning
brushing sand
from between the sheets

bowing low
beneath the maple branches
heavy rain

the sun's warmth
store front mannequins
also changing clothes

summer storm
at the nape of her neck
a single curl

washing up
smell of the campfire
rising with the steam

summer's end
wild raspberries
dried on the stem

moonviewing party
the children stand
out in the rain

after the ambulance
still waiting
for his key in the lock

resting her head
on the shoulder strap
the long ride home

autumn rain—
wells in the limestone
beneath the drip tiles

approaching winter
the last of the gingko trees
caught in the pine

early darkness
bookmarking "winter"
in my saijiki

cluster of berries
beyond my fingers
clear blue skies

Bachini
Chang
Connor
Elliott
Giesecke
Gilliland
gordon
Howard
Jensen

Kaur

Ketchek
Lippy
Missias
Ogoshi
Partridge
Patrick
Rohrig
Stefanac
Watsky
Young

Harsangeet Kaur
Homemaker

Born 17 May 1967
Johor Bahru, Malaysia
Currently resides
Singapore

Kaur writes of her family and neighborhood without sentimentality—no small achievement. In this vein her voice emerges as quiet and domestic. Often, however, she catches the color and drama of her native surroundings with a flair and precision that makes even the exotic seem familiar to the reader. These moments connect with our own lives and neighborhoods, regardless of the hemispere or continent from which they derive.

Credits

monsoon: *unpublished*
nose pressed to the window: *unpublished*
little fingers caressed: *unpublished*
through the cigarette smoke: *unpublished*
quiet conversation: *unpublished*
slowly his finger: *unpublished*
plastic lawn mower: *unpublished*
calling his sister: *unpublished*
church bells: *unpublished*
rickshaw: *unpublished*
evening downpour: *unpublished*
silent night: *unpublished*
searching for nits: *unpublished*
long distance call: *unpublished*
winter evening: *unpublished*

monsoon—
the fresh paint
lies in puddles

nose pressed to the window
he watches his grandpa
change hair colour

little fingers caress
  the dividing lines
    —completed jigsaw

through the cigarette smoke
a young woman
makes eyes at my daughter

quiet conversation—
her hand reaches out
to smooth the tablecloth

slowly his finger
  translates the old song
for his granddaughter

plastic lawn mower
moving in the same line
as daddy

calling his sister
  his eyes don't leave
    the ant trail . . .

church bells—
another car
parks illegally

rickshaw—
one old man offers a ride
to another

evening downpour:
in the old quarry
the water changes colour

silent night—
the neighbor's cat
pauses at my open door

searching for nits
the first
gray hair

long distance call—
my daughter tells me
she has hurt her knee

winter evening . . .
your letters crowding
the little board

Bachini
Chang
Connor
Elliott
Giesecke
Gilliland
gordon
Howard
Jensen
Kaur

Ketchek

Lippy
Missias
Ogoshi
Partridge
Patrick
Rohrig
Stefanac
Watsky
Young

Michael Ketchek

Day Care Teacher

Born 9 July 1954
Detroit, Michigan
Currently resides
Rochester, New York

Ketchek's work reminds us repeatedly that the poet has met the world with optimism, been disabused of ideals, yet has emerged from this experience with a keen sense of life's compensations. The larger issues of living may not be within our control, but the small moments are reward enough. *Going on* is the theme, made possible in the end by a glimpse of something unexpected and renewing.

Credits

light morning mist: *Modern Haiku XIX:3*
the sparkle: *Raw NervZ IV:1*
afternoon café: *South by Southeast 5:2*
ten minutes to five: *Modern Haiku XXII:2*
my father: *Frogpond XX:3*
thinking about: *Frogpond XX:1*
really angry: *Raw NervZ III:3*
gunfire: *Modern Haiku XXVIII:3*
pausing to gaze at: *black bough 2*
rust poking through: *Brussels Sprout X:1*
gentle breeze: *Raw NervZ IV:4*
two fishermen: *Frogpond XIII:1*
small piece of chocolate: *Brussels Sprout X:3*
autumn leaves: *Modern Haiku XXX:1*
one more spring: *Modern Haiku XXIII:3*

light morning mist & *ten minutes to five*
both appeared in *Haiku Moment*
pausing to gaze at appeared in *Road Work*
one more spring appeared in *Haiku World*

light morning mist
only the roller coaster
rises above the trees

the sparkle
in the grass where
the creek got loose

afternoon café
the captured chessmen
in an empty cup

ten minutes to five
the goldfish
swim back and forth

my father
losing his memory
asks me not to forget him

thinking about
mindfulness
I pee on my shoe

really angry
the haiku poet
writes free verse

gunfire
looking back and forth
from tv to window

pausing to gaze at
the storm damaged tree
boxer doing roadwork

rust poking through
the flower decal
VW bus

gentle breeze
marijuana smoke drifts
through me

two fishermen
respectfully watching
the heron

small piece of chocolate
melting in my mouth
Indian Summer day

autumn leaves
floating on the pond
one last swim

one more spring
part of the cherry tree
in bloom

Bachini

Chang

Connor

Elliott

Giesecke

Gilliland

gordon

Howard

Jensen

Kaur

Ketchek

Lippy

Missias

Ogoshi

Partridge

Patrick

Rohrig

Stefanac

Watsky

Young

Burnell Lippy
Apple Picker

Born 16 April 1944
Manchester, Maryland
Currently resides
Mt Tremper, New York

Lippy's work can be seen as a form of meditation, a means of being present in the world—or better, of living it directly. The poet feels sharply the most basic elements: heat and cold, wet and dry, light and dark. These are the chief actors, with the secondary players—mice, cows, turtles, the occasional human—shown primarily in reaction to these larger forces.

Credits

the village postmaster: *unpublished*
the end of a log: *unpublished*
a bumblebee: *unpublished*
summer afternoon: *unpublished*
summer storm: *Frogpond XXI:3*
a lure: *Frogpond XXI:3*
smell of the papers: *unpublished*
cold morning: *Frogpond XXI:1*
freezing rain: *Modern Haiku XXVIII:3*
the night's single car: *unpublished*
such a cold night: *unpublished*
the shortest night: *unpublished*
late winter light: *Modern Haiku XXVIII:3*
winter rain: *unpublished*
getting up to pee: *unpublished*

the village postmaster
not noticing my presence—
Main Street's deep shade

the end of a log
still wet from a turtle—
summer moon

a bumblebee brushes
the window's torn screen—
back room coolness

summer afternoon—
the sunken log's
angle of refraction

summer storm—
the haytruck's mirror
drags a branch

a lure
reeled through pads—
August afternoon

smell of the papers
brought inside—
cold autumn rain

cold morning—
mouse tracks
across a pan's old lard

freezing rain—
the long hallway
of a closed school

the night's single car
rotten ice
the whole length of the lake

such a cold night
the uneven stones
of the walk

the shortest night—
sated lovers
eating with their fingers

late winter light—
the recycled paper
of a seed catalogue

winter rain—
the shed's last firewood
slips loose of its bark

getting up to pee
on the dark side of the house—
full winter moon

Bachini

Chang

Connor

Elliott

Giesecke

Gilliland

gordon

Howard

Jensen

Kaur

Ketchek

Lippy

Missias

Ogoshi

Partridge

Patrick

Rohrig

Stefanac

Watsky

Young

A. C. Missias

Biologist

Born 26 May 1967
Naha, Okinawa
Currently resides
Philadelphia, Pennsylvania

The parameters of Missias' world emerge clearly from these poems: orderly, full of familiar beings and objects, within which she is at ease and able to notice the ineffable in the ordinary. It is not free of darkness, however, for there is a strong suggestion of *memento mori* in this work. Under the seeming calm, she is capable of great range: instances of death and regeneration, the nuances of human relationship, the scope and power of natural forces.

Credits

park chessboard: *Frogpond XXII:1*
autumn rain: *Frogpond XXI:1*
three broken pots: *black bough 12*
winter evening: *unpublished*
again I choose: *unpublished*
winter dawn: *Frogpond XXII:1*
lake cottage: *Frogpond XXI:2*
summer rain: *Frogpond XXII:2*
roadside fence: *Frogpond XXI:3*
silent train: *Persimmon II:2*
winter playground: *Frogpond XXI:1*
home from the funeral: *Modern Haiku XXIX:2*
spring rain: *Frogpond XXII:2*
new grave: *Modern Haiku XXIX:1*
city park: *Herb Barrett Contest Anthology*

city park won 2nd Prize in the Herb Barrett Contest 1998

park chessboard—
rain caught
in the missing squares

autumn rain—
the weathered tire swing
  overflows

three broken pots
coming from the kiln
  and then that bowl

winter evening—
the neighbor's lawn chairs
in a tight circle

again I choose
not to dial your number
  the cat's tight curl

winter dawn—
leaning into
the mare's warm flank

lake cottage—
the wicker chair seats
giving way

summer rain—
on top of the sheets
we lie without touching

roadside fence—
the pony briefly
keeping pace

silent train
the man ahead of me also
watches the darkness

winter playground—
  the boy's face lost
    behind his shouts

home from the funeral—
pausing to knock the earth
from his shoes

spring rain—
around the feeder
sunflowers

new grave—
the trampled grass
already recovering

city park—
the wind takes a leaf
from the chessboard

Bachini

Chang

Connor

Elliott

Giesecke

Gilliland

gordon

Howard

Jensen

Kaur

Ketchek

Lippy

Missias

Ogoshi

Partridge

Patrick

Rohrig

Stefanac

Watsky

Young

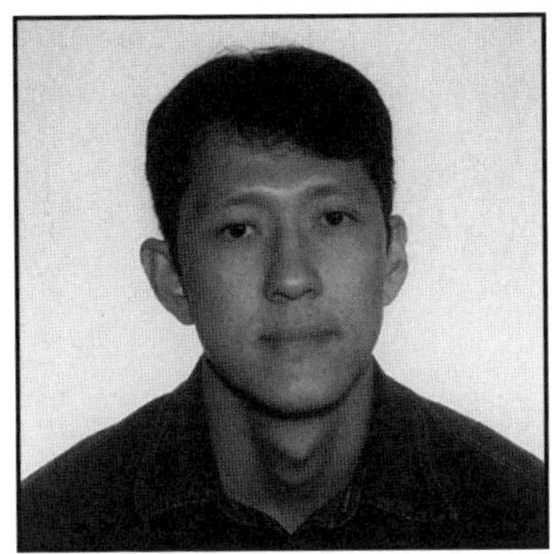

Fumio Ogoshi
Graduate Student

Born 1 February 1972
Nara, Japan
Currently resides
Irvine, California

What is immediate in Ogoshi's work is the acuity of his observations—a sense that we have encountered another scale of things. He brings this facility to bear most tellingly in his observations of people, and it is here we find his most distinct voice: slight amusement, and a growing empathy. We recognise the predicaments of his subjects, have ourselves felt the sting of their small humiliations.

Credits

spring bloom: *unpublished*
faint voices of neighbors: *unpublished*
after the story: *unpublished*
a quiet lakeshore: *unpublished*
autumn wind: *Frogpond XXII:2*
New Year's morning: *Haiku Headlines*
unbearable heat: *unpublished*
along a grapevine: *unpublished*
rainbow fragments: *unpublished*
a broken flower pot: *unpublished*
a school of fish: *black bough 12*
returning an umbrella: *unpublished*
lost child: *unpublished*
sneezing in church: *Heron Quarterly 2:1*
peeling an orange: *unpublished*

spring bloom—
a young girl singing
beyond her range

faint voices of neighbors—
only understanding
their laughs

after the story—
a slow cough, cough
for an ending

quiet lakeshore—
each wave overcome
by the next

autumn wind—
licking a bum's hand
a stray dog

New Year's morning:
finding snow
in the dumpster

unbearable heat—
seen through a window
white roses

along a grape vine—
sunlight reflected
off backs of ants

rainbow fragments—
shifting from sprinkler
to sprinkler

a broken flower pot—
sunlight leaking
through the cracks

a school of fish
following the clouds—
coolness

returning an umbrella—
stepping into a puddle
hidden by my shadow

lost child—
clinging onto the legs
of a mannequin

sneezing in church—
no one said
"bless you"

peeling an orange—
the sourness
before the taste

Bachini
Chang
Connor
Elliott
Giesecke
Gilliland
gordon
Howard
Jensen
Kaur
Ketchek
Lippy
Missias
Ogoshi

Partridge

Patrick
Rohrig
Stefanac
Watsky
Young

Brent Partridge

Gardener

Born 21 August 1953
Anchorage, Alaska
Currently resides
Berkeley, California

Partridge shows a practiced hand and an evolved style that reflect his many years of writing haiku, including long periods in Japan. His work might be considered the most objective in this volume, and the most tinged with a Zen perspective. Things are seen as they are, and he writes exactly as he sees, without inflating or dramatizing—almost without a trace of his own personality. This clean look at the world is refreshing, and appealing in a subliminal and fundamental way.

Credits

a snowy daybreak: *Frogpond XIX:3*
the coldest season: *Frogpond XX:3*
rest of the world: *Modern Haiku XXIII:3*
many of the godwits: *Frogpond XIX:1*
crabapple blooming: *Modern Haiku XXVIII:3*
even in dreams: *Modern Haiku XX:3*
a wet evening: *Frogpond XVIII:2*
across the courtyard: *Inkstone 4:2*
cutting flowers after dark: *Dragonfly 14:3*
redwoods: *Modern Haiku XX:2*
fountain catching light: *Mainichi Daily News #588*
the autumn colors: *Frogpond XX:2*
hail in the woods: *Modern Haiku XX:3*
burning the wood: *Frogpond XIII:4*
Eskimo mask: *Frogpond XVII:1*

a snowy daybreak—
everything's just different
shades of violet

the coldest season
and even my eyebrows
are getting thinner

rest of the world
arranged around it—
plum tree in bloom

many of the godwits
hopping on one leg—
the spring wind

crabapple blooming—
in its lower middle
the sparrows' quickie

even in dreams
quite alone
late spring rain

a wet evening—
the chill of the cherries is
part of their flavor

across the courtyard
osprey on another tower
   looking out to sea

cutting flowers after dark:
brushing against each other
dahlias squeak

redwoods
sopping up
the fog

fountain catching light
the transparency
of October air

the autumn colors
and just the foundation
of an old farmhouse

hail in the woods
my maul and hammer
ring

burning the wood
of a tree
struck by lightning

Eskimo mask
takes on color
during the storm

Bachini
Chang
Connor
Elliott
Giesecke
Gilliland
gordon
Howard
Jensen
Kaur
Ketchek
Lippy
Missias
Ogoshi
Partridge

Patrick

Rohrig
Stefanac
Watsky
Young

Carl Patrick

College Professor

Born 2 July 1937
Houston, Texas
Currently resides
Brooklyn, New York

The surfaces of Patrick's poems present no threat. Indeed, they are commonplace images from everyday life. But lurking behind these placid exteriors is a taste for the wild, the chaotic, the unformed, which provides the tang for his best work. Only in reference to this underworld can we explain the energy that drives these seemingly simple poems beyond urban myth to the realm of felt truth.

Credits

late at night: *unpublished*
soft spring night: *unpublished*
no one for miles: *unpublished*
I fall asleep: *unpublished*
sound of rain: *unpublished*
after ringing it up: *Absence of Cows*
angry with my son: *Frogpond XXI:2*
the nightlight glows: *In the Waterfall*
coolness at dusk: *unpublished*
late autumn: *unpublished*
squeezing her breasts: *unpublished*
at the fruitstand: *In the Waterfall*
first cold night: *After Lights Out*
reflected in: *After Lights Out*
fireflies: *The Red Moon Anthology 1998*

at the fruitstand & first cold night
appeared in *The Haiku Anthology*
fireflies won 1st Prize in the 1998 Brady Senryu Contest

late at night
opening the refrigerator
rows of white eggs

soft spring night
the sound of a dog
lapping water

no one for miles
moonlit dew
on the mailbox

I fall asleep
thinking of the
watermelon cooling

sound of rain
in the cat's
eyes

after ringing it up
the cashier sniffs
my sprig of mint

angry with my son
I discuss it first
with the tulips

the nightlight glows
on the rim of
mother's wheelchair

coolness at dusk
the swaying of long stalks
of wild garlic

late autumn
the blue pilot light
in the gas heater

squeezing her breasts
while the eggs
boil

at the fruitstand
I take off my mitten
to feel the coconut

first cold night
the fat tomcat hangs from
the window screen

reflected in
the cop's dark shades
fireworks

fireflies
my neighbor
has more

Bachini
Chang
Connor
Elliott
Giesecke
Gilliland
gordon
Howard
Jensen
Kaur
Ketchek
Lippy
Missias
Ogoshi
Partridge
Patrick

Rohrig

Stefanac
Watsky
Young

Carolyne Rohrig

Born 1 May 1950
Buenos Aires, Argentina
Currently resides
Fremont, California

The poet's voice in these selections shows no illusions about life. This is not Shangri-la; we grow older and take on responsibility. Yet Rohrig's subjects have the resources for coping with these difficult truths. There is always a response, a way of carrying on—an underlying optimism. These people and these poems gather strength from being able to include their all, past and present, in engaging the future.

Credits

graduation speech: *Haiku Canada Sheet*
gone swimming: *unpublished*
pregnant: *unpublished*
the dog growls: *Haiku Canada Newsletter XI:3*
cloudy skies: *Modern Haiku XXIX:2*
kicking stones: *unpublished*
job interview: *unpublished*
get-well balloon: *unpublished*
walking on needles: *black bough 10*
field mice: *The Scare Crow*
chemotherapy: *unpublished*
digging ditches: *unpublished*
afternoon break: *unpublished*
late night at the airport: *unpublished*
merry-go-round: *Modern Haiku XXIX:3*

graduation speech—
the seniors twirl
their tassels

gone swimming—
I slip into the warmth
of your lounge chair

pregnant—
sucking at her feet
the outgoing tide

the dog growls
at the wetsuit
hanging up to dry

cloudy skies—
different shades of shadow
in the cauliflower

kicking stones
on the trail
the lump in my breast

job interview—
therapist's son
makes no eye contact

get-well balloon
losing air every day—
the long journey home

walking on needles
in the forest—
your silence

field mice—
the scarecrow's head
drooping lower

chemotherapy
drying in the dish rack
her long-haired wig

digging ditches—
dirt in the crease
of his stomach

afternoon break—
the fused-glass artist pours
honey in the tea

late night at the airport
the shoe shine man
polishing his own shoes

merry-go-round
the one-eyed horse
rides empty

Bachini
Chang
Connor
Elliott
Giesecke
Gilliland
gordon
Howard
Jensen
Kaur
Ketchek
Lippy
Missias
Ogoshi
Partridge
Patrick
Rohrig

Stefanac

Watsky
Young

R. A. Stefanac
Gallery Manager

Born 30 July 1935
Pittsburgh, Pennsylvania
Currently resides
Pittsburgh, Pennsylvania

Stefanac's poems here are fraught with a consciousness of desire and need, and often with the unsatisfactory nature of their temporary satiation. There is a weight of consequence to the choices offered to him, which amassed are palpably oppressive. Only in diversion—a ballgame, perhaps—does this burden lighten. In this he recognizes the value of the struggle, and the necessity of a snatched leisure which equips him for it.

Credits

ballgame: *Raw NervZ III:2*
hunter's moon: *Raw NervZ V:3*
blind date: *Modern Haiku XXIX:2*
unprotected sex: *Raw NervZ V:1*
Christmas past: *Woodnotes 27*
a flashback: *Frogpond XXI:3*
adding weight: *Modern Haiku XXVIII:2*
steady rain: *black bough 11*
lovers' moon: *Raw NervZ III:4*
liaison: *Raw NervZ III:4*
a falling star: *Raw NervZ V:1*
frost predicted: *Mayfly 24*
thrift shop: *Raw NervZ IV:4*
dad's wake: *Mayfly 22*
alone: *South by Southeast 4:1*

ballgame & *dad's wake* both appeared in *The Red Moon Anthology 1996*
alone appeared in *The Red Moon Anthology 1997*

ballgame
catching the curve
of the peanut vendor

hunter's moon
the overflow crowd
at the singles bar

blind date
the sugar cube taking time
to dissolve

unprotected sex
the steady tick
of the ceiling fan

Christmas past
the pine needles
under the rug

a flashback
of childhood abuse
  Uncle Al's aftershave

adding weight
to the bending peony
—black ants

steady rain
a crossing guard
hunches her shoulders

lovers' moon
   opening
a foil-wrapped condom

liaison
   stripping
the double bed

falling star   we talk abortion

frost predicted
  the sizzle
of fried green tomatoes

thrift shop
the winter overcoat
one size too small

dad's wake
  the weight
of my new shoes

alone . . .
a downdraft
stirs the ashes

Bachini

Chang

Connor

Elliott

Giesecke

Gilliland

gordon

Howard

Jensen

Kaur

Ketchek

Lippy

Missias

Ogoshi

Partridge

Patrick

Rohrig

Stefanac

Watsky

Young

Paul Watsky
Psychiatrist

Born 13 August 1943
New York, New York
Currently resides
San Francisco, California

Pure irony generally makes for weak haiku: it is too cold, too knowing to stir the reader's empathetic response. But Watsky's often ironic voice is tempered by a benevolent eye, and his range of sympathies is seemingly inexhaustible. This does not compromise his sharpness of observation, however, or his ability to enjoy and share a good laugh, which happily is often.

Credits

New Year's afternoon: *unpublished*
early summer: *Frogpond XXI:3*
harbor evening: *Hummingbird*
early appointment: *South by Southeast 4:1*
coffee house window: *unpublished*
science museum: *Frogpond XXII:3*
late April: *Hummingbird VII:3*
spring breeze: *Heron Quarterly II:2*
water park Sunday: *unpublished*
carrying their canes: *Frogpond XX:2*
his ashes scattered: *Frogpond XIX:3*
sunny afternoon: *unpublished*
high window sill: *Frogpond XIX:1*
World Cup summer: *Frogpond XXII:2*
looking back and forth: *Modern Haiku XXVII:1*

his ashes scattered appeared in *The Red Moon Anthology 1996*
early appointment & *carrying their canes*
both appeared in *The Red Moon Anthology 1997*
science museum appeared in *The Red Moon Anthology 1998*

New Year's afternoon—
sleeping off our hangovers
beneath the same quilt

early summer—
a rotten doormat hung
on the guest house fence

harbor evening—
in the old schooner's wheelhouse
two play scrabble

early appointment—
the analyst's office full
of yesterday's heat

coffee house window—
a young beauty reading
Crime and Punishment

science museum—
men's room towel dispenser
jammed

late April—
calves stampeding
past the quiet cows

spring breeze—
child stomping
a paper scrap

water park Sunday—
my kids vanish into
a sea of people

carrying their canes
two old women lean
on each other

his ashes scattered
what to do
with the box

sunny afternoon—
my tongue explores the new cap
on a broken tooth

high window sill—
teetering towards birdsong
my arthritic cat

World Cup summer—
ball idle, three boys argue
on the damp lawn

looking back and forth—
the borrowed tent spread out
wrinkled instructions

Bachini
Chang
Connor
Elliott
Giesecke
Gilliland
gordon
Howard
Jensen
Kaur
Ketchek
Lippy
Missias
Ogoshi
Partridge
Patrick
Rohrig
Stefanac
Watsky

Young

Laura Young

Materials Creator

Born 21 June 1962
Louisville, Kentucky
Currently resides
Monticello, Florida

When we see the range of subject, emotion, and circumstance which this poet offers, it is impossible not to consider that she has lived a full and eventful life, and has observed well and often along the way. Most importantly, however, she has retained the ability to observe herself from without, recognising also the foreignness of self in a world grown familiar through experience.

Credits

sea oats: *Fuyoh*
summer morning: *Raw NervZ VI:2*
busy in the garden: *Haiku in the Light*
watermelon juice: *unpublished*
blue leatherette: *Modern Haiku XXVIII:3*
morning fog: *Frogpond XX:3*
spring burial: *Modern Haiku XXVIII:3*
new mushroom: *From a Kind Neighbor*
with each crash: *unpublished*
the child's slow breath: *Tundra 1*
the answering machine: *unpublished*
month of night: *unpublished*
the short day: *unpublished*
firelight: *unpublished*
time to dig: *unpublished*

sea oats—
all day the nesting peacock
swivels her head

summer morning
the mutt licks up
the biscuit-scented air

busy in the garden . . .
a kink in the hose
pulls a weed

watermelon juice
slips down my wrist—
taste of sweat

blue leatherette—
how foreign I look in my
passport photograph

morning fog—
lifting an earflap
to judge the coyote howls

spring burial
the twin stands up to give
his eulogy

new mushroom
a clod of dirt
on its cap

with each crash
the sound of the chainsaw
clearer

the child's slow breath
stays the hand closing in
to turn the page

the answering machine
playing mother's voice too slowly
  winter light

month of night—
a neighbor reading mail
by carlight

the short day—
a woodpile grows
on the porch

firelight—
thawing out the top layer
of their wedding cake

time to dig
the sweet potatoes
still no news from you